He Can,
He Will,
He Did.

Written by: Stevie Lewis

ISBN: 979-8-89786-013-5

Table of Contents

Foreword

"If you ever question whether God cares deeply for you, open this book," My daughter Stevie "reminds us that we are never alone, or without hope or help because we have a miracle-working God who works alongside us and lifts us out of storms." Bob Goff wrote this statement to endorse a book of renowned author Max Lucado, but I also believe it to be true of the book you hold in your hands.

My daughter, Stevie, has witnessed a miracle from God after daily prayers and her faithfulness in God. Stevie has put up with 16 years of having a seizure disorder and dealing with 7-10 seizures daily, as this started at 5 months old. Stevie always had faith that God would heal her. Stevie loves effortlessly and is appreciative of her days being seizure free. Stevie experienced at an early age that her life was different from others. She had to put up with never knowing when the seizures would occur, or how many seizures she would have in a day and night.

As a mother, I limited Stevie on what she could do, as I was always trying to protect her from falling due to a seizure. She broke her nose twice at school from seizures and was my special angel baby that I felt I needed to protect. Stevie put up with peers at school being rude, never knowing when her seizures would oc-cur, being a spectacle during her seizures, two broken nose incidences, and just being different from the norm. Her seizures happened all day long, no rhyme or reason, and even through the night. She would go to sleep having seizures, get woken up at night with them, have them every morning in her bed, then again all throughout the day.

Life was "normal" and fine between sei-zures, but it broke my heart to see her having seizures. It was just a part of her life that she had seizures. When God healed Stevie, she was 16 years old, just like she always said. Stevie went through her life of seizures with the best attitude and gratitude for God. She has always been so faithful and Stevie's faith in God fa-cilitated the final results of her miracle: that when she turned 16 years old, God did take her seizures away forever because she knew, and would tell me, "I will be healed in God's time".

After we tried to have brain surgery at 16 years old, we found out that she could NOT be a candidate for surgery, as there was a spot on her brain that the seizures originated from and that spot was too close to the movement of her legs and the memory and language portion of her brain. So, the doctors declared her condition to be inoperable. She would not be able to walk or talk after surgery. That was just the reality that we had to face. She wanted her independence and wanted to be able to drive a car. Then on August 13, 2019 she was 16 years old and she had her LAST seizure, THANKS BE TO GOD!!!   She came home from a restaurant to study and get ready for bed, and she had a seizure in the yard getting out of the car with my husband. That was the LAST time she had a seizure. None through the night, none in the morning, and none the next day at school!! It was a miracle!! NO SEIZURES again!!

After 16 years of being disabled with epilepsy, Stevie's belief and patience in God's healing came to a reality for her. Stevie has truly experienced a miracle from our GOD, and there are not enough words to express how much we appreciate it. Stevie got her driver's license 6 months later and has now gone off to college, is working a job, and is driving her car every day!

We thank God daily for his miracles in our lives. Faith has lifted us out of Stevie's storms of life! God is with us, and He will perform miracles through FAITH! You just have to believe and ask Him!! We thank You and we love You Jesus!! THANKS BE TO GOD!

What a privilege to introduce you to my daughter Stevie Leigh Lewis.

~ Katherine Flournoy Lindsey

Chapter 1: Insight to life

On May 18, 2003, a baby girl was born in Jacksonville, Florida. Little did she know what lay ahead of her. She was named Stevie Leigh Lewis. Her middle name came from her mom's cousin Leigh, the labor doctor when her mom gave birth to her. Stevie's parents are David and Katherine Lewis. Stevie has dark brown hair with light brown eyes that match the leaves in the fall. Stevie had a head full of soft, wavy dark brown hair that always seemed to catch the sunlight just right — turning it into a halo of warm chestnut at the edges. Her eyes were large and expressive, a unique shade of light brown that shimmered like fallen autumn leaves, rich with gold and amber flecks.

Her skin was a soft olive tone, smooth and glowing with a warmth that made her eyes seem even brighter. Strangers would often comment on how large and beautiful her eyes were. She didn't smile for just anyone — Stevie was incredibly particular, clinging tightly to her mother or grandma and wailing when anyone else tried to hold her. "A mama's girl through and through," her mom would say with a laugh, though secretly she cherished how fiercely Stevie wanted only her.

Her mother always said Stevie was the most beautiful baby she had ever seen — not just for her looks but because she had this calm intensity about her. She seemed to watch the world, taking it in before acting, almost as if she understood more than she should. She always stayed close — never one to wander too far, never one to jump into a stranger's arms.

At only five months old, I , Stevie, was diagnosed with epilepsy. It didn't take long before the diagnosis became a lifelong reality. My mom and I had just gone to the kitchen for breakfast when she set me on the counter in my baby seat and rushed to the bedroom to get her slippers. At that moment, I had a febrile seizure. Mom returned from the bedroom to experience it with me. Of course, she was in shock and under immense stress, since at this time we were home alone. She was in complete worry as at that moment the entire situation felt like it was in her hands. During the seizure, I turned blue from the lack of oxygen in my lungs. My mom rushed me to the emergency room. As we were driving to the hospital tears rolled down her cheeks out of worry for my survival and safety. She just prayed to the Lord that everything would turn out okay and that I would be in good health. Her tears continued to fall as she sank in the waiting room chair and looked into my eyes. It felt like her world was falling apart as her baby girl was experiencing this awful seizure.

The doctors initially believed it was just a febrile seizure, but then a few weeks passed and I had another. Then, after that, I was diagnosed with epilepsy. During my seizures at that age, my right shoulder would twitch and my eyes would blink rapidly. As an infant, I had six to twelve seizures a day. Little did I know at the time how difficult this journey would become or how it would positively impact my life. Throughout this book, I will share my journey with seizures and explain how living with epilepsy has ultimately benefited my life and shaped me into the person I am today.

The type of epilepsy I was diagnosed with was called tonic-clonic epilepsy. It involves tonic (stiffening) and clonic (twitching or jerking) phases of muscle activity. These types of seizures typically start with an aura, or partial seizure, which is the feeling someone gets before the seizure begins. An aura is the warning to sit down before the seizure begins. I had a spot on the left side of my brain, which is also known as focal cortical dysplasia, that caused the seizures. For any of those who may not know exactly what focal cortical dysplasia means, it is a congenital abnormality of brain development, where the neurons in the brain fail to migrate properly in that specific area, which is formed in utero. My epilepsy developed approximately two weeks into term when my mom was pregnant with me. They never found the exact cause of the development of my epilepsy. At the time we only knew that it was something that we were going to have to normalize. While it's hard to see the ones we love go through hard times or difficulty, I am here to share that it also isn't easy being the one to go through them.

A few known causes of seizures are highly emotional situations, stress, lack of sleep, not eating enough, and anything sudden. These causes give rise to an unbalanced electrical current through the brain, causing a seizure, also known as a convulsion. For example, something as simple as a fire drill in school often caused me to go into a seizure. I was given accommodation to go outside before the fire drill started or at least be notified that it was going to happen soon. In the field, I would have to lay down and wait until the seizure passed. Then,

I would return to the line where the rest of my classmates were. During each seizure I had the tendency to try to grab onto things to help keep myself in control.

Also, once my leg would begin to jerk, I would try to lift my leg back up which felt like a million pounds in the moment. I lifted my leg up so when my leg would jerk it could go down, instead of staying in the same position during the whole duration of the seizure. That actually helped me feel more in control. Why did I need to be in control or want to feel in control? The desire for control often stems from a deep-seated need for security and pre-dictability in an unpredictable world. It can be comforting to believe that we have the power to influence our circumstances, providing a sense of stability amidst chaos. Predictability and security were something I lacked while living with seizures, since I never knew when my next seizure was going to happen. Every-where I went, I would look around in search of somewhere to go in case a seizure did occur. My seizures made me sad because during the time they were happening I had close to no control over my body. No matter where we were, if I felt a seizure coming on I would have to lay down wherever I was at the moment- whether that be a parking deck, grocery store, bathroom, etc. Having almost no control over your body is terrifying especially in unfamiliar places.

My doctor recommended brain surgery when I was three years old. While at the Children's Hospital in Augusta, Georgia, we thought about getting the surgery. Even though there was a seventy percent chance that it would work and a thirty percent chance that it wouldn't, my mother was hesitant about the whole situation. The surgery came at a high risk of memory loss and difficulty processing auditory information, because the spot on my brain that was causing the seizures was located on the left temporal lobe. I can't imagine the immense stress and sorrow my mom was experiencing at the time. All she wanted was for me to be okay, but at that time God had other plans for me. His plans for me included experiencing this difficulty, which has made me into the extremely strong individual I am today.

We were advised not to proceed with the surgery by Pa, my grandfather, Dr. Edwin Elliott Flournoy, who was a medical doctor. The stakes were so high that I could come out of surgery not knowing how to communicate, forgetting who I knew, including myself, or not making much sense. Also, there was a chance that after they cracked open my skull, completed the surgery, and stitched me back up, my face would never go back to its original size; as it was predicted to swell to twice its normal size. The decision was made by my mom and Pa as my parents were separated and my dad was not present at the time. The seventy percent success rate was too risky, and they decided not to do the surgery.

While I was at the hospital, the nurses had to take some of my blood, and since I was so young and my arms were so little it was hard for them to find a vein to stick. They had to stick my arm several times then switch to the other arm to find a better vein and stuck that arm several times before they found a good vein. The nurse wrapped gauze around both of my arms from where they had been stuck. When the nurse left the room I said, "Look, Mama, they broke both of my arms," and tears started to fall from my Mom's eyes. I also had gauze wrapped around my head to hold the wires for the EEG in place. Yet another hard moment for a mom to have to go through. My mom wrapped her arms and her head around in gauze, then did the same to my baby doll so I wouldn't feel alone.

24 Hour EEG

So what exactly is an EEG? An EEG is an electroencephalogram, which measures the electrical activity to the brain. The point of the EEG was for when I had a seizure they could then measure the unbalanced electrical current in my brain that was causing my seizures. From a very young age seizures became part of who I am. Every time I had a seizure, there was pain to my leg from all my muscles spasming throughout the seizure and the uncontrollable jerking of my right leg that could possibly lead to injury. To explain what a seizure feels like, imagine every muscle in your body working against each other and the pain it would cause. Although, it was more mentally painful than physically.

In this type of epilepsy, I would stay conscious the entire time, so I could feel everything. I felt the jerking of my whole right leg, sometimes even my entire body. I could feel myself not having any control over my body, which was extremely upsetting. I would have three to six seizures a day, each lasting approximately five minutes.

As I got older, my seizures became worse, but I never lost my faith in God. People would ask me how I had such a positive mindset about my situation, and my answer was always, "Because I know God will heal me."

A Promise I Carried

My faith was rooted in me from my grandparents. They both glowed in faith. Every morning when I spent the night at their house we would do our morning devotional together. Being so young, I would only read the thought for the day, while my grandma would read the prayer, and my grandpa would say the day's devotion. As I got older my grandpa let me start reading the devotional and the more I studied the Bible the more my faith grew. They led me to faith and made my faith stronger each day. My grandpa was a Bible study teacher and would study the Bible often. He and my grandma were and will always be my role models. The kind of love they had for each other showed that God put them together. I pray that one day I'll find a love that resembles what they had.

There will always be times that you feel down in life. But because of what my grandparents taught me, I believe there's no reason to think the worst or be depressed. You must live your life to the fullest, no matter the problems you face. "Dream as if you'll live forever; live as if you'll die today." Every day was hard, but I persevered through it. After every seizure, my mom would say, "I wish God would take these seizures away." I always responded, "Mom, He will in His own time. When I am sixteen, God is going to take these seizures away." I started to say "Mom, He will in His own time," at the age of seven. I just knew it wasn't going to last forever. I could feel it in my bones and and in my heart that by the time I was sixteen years old God would heal me.

Because of this, I knew I would be able to achieve my goal of being able to drive. If you believe in God fully and truly, He will perform miracles. If you keep your faith and believe that He will relieve you from life's struggles, He will heal you from the struggles you face. By keeping the faith and believing in God, you shall be healed. Psalm 30:2 says "Lord, my God, I called to You for help, and You healed me."

Invisible Battles

In my younger years, I would lock myself in the bathroom, often sinking to the floor in agony. There is no doubt the pain was emotionally and physically tearing me apart. I don't remember every episode I've had, but the ones that stood out the most happened in the shower. Everything is slick, making it impossible to maintain control of your body. Having a seizure in the shower makes you more susceptible to injury. Even though no one in my life knew, I had seizures in the shower all this time. Everyone close to me tried to understand what I was going through, but, in all honesty, no one will ever understand the impact seizures have had on my life.

Back then, I felt extremely alone because no one could understand what it felt like to go through seizures on a daily basis. I never met anyone who could truly relate to me because even everyone that I knew with epilepsy had a different type of epilepsy. I felt alone in this big world, but I knew God was there beside me through it all. God made me into the person I am today. I would never want to erase the struggles throughout my life because they sculpted and strengthened me.

Behind all the struggles I faced, there was a reason for it all. As I was growing up, God always made me stronger. I couldn't physically feel His presence, but when I would say my daily prayers to Him, I felt a sense of warmth as if He was sitting right there with me, holding me tightly in His arms, reminding me that every-thing was going to be okay.

I believe if the hardships people face throughout their lives didn't happen, they would turn out to be completely different people. If I had never had seizure disorder, I wouldn't be who I am now. Never question your life, no matter how bad it may seem at the moment. Trust me, God has a plan for you. When I was growing up, and still to this day, I always told myself, "Think positive, and don't let anyone bring you down." Even though my seizures felt really hard for me, I didn't let the problems get me down. I was constantly smiling through all the pain.

In my opinion, there is no reason not to smile; life will always get better eventually. I like the quote, "Always find a reason to smile." I never let my demons win. I persevered through life, growing up with a smile and living my life to the fullest potential. I didn't like how peo-ple would tell me I couldn't do something just because of my epilepsy.

No one ever realized the restraints I had throughout life, I was never allowed to go any-where alone. Even when we went to the Grand Canyon, I was cautioned not to get too close to the edge to avoid any injuries. I never shared my sorrows with my family members or close friends because I knew these restraints were for my own safety, but they also kept me from truly feeling like a kid. Everything I did I would second guess and make sure it was safe, or I would plan out where I would lay down next if I were to have a seizure. I made it my responsibility to protect the ones I love by trying to hide my seizures because I could see the sadness in their eyes when I would experience one. All I wanted was to see the ones I love be happy.

As a young child, I couldn't speak up for myself because that would cause high emotion that resulted in a seizure. My leg would jerk uncontrollably and start to ache from the muscles moving against each other constantly. Since I couldn't speak up for myself without the chance of having a seizure, I just became quiet. I talked to very few people at school because there were a lot of kids who made fun of me for being different.

I kept to myself throughout the years I had epilepsy. I felt almost as if I didn't have a voice, like a shadow of a person because no one seemed to see me as an equal.

It felt like I was watching the world through a lens. There were times that I felt unseen. As if I was just there watching the world move around me as I was stuck in a safety bubble of restrictions and limitations meant for my protection.

I wasn't allowed to go on roller coasters because my mom and I were both nervous about what would happen if I were to have a seizure during the ride. I also was not able to stay up late to hangout with friends because if I didn't get enough sleep it would cause more prevalent seizures the next day. I was not able to play laser tag because of the lights, adrenaline, and sudden movements (a warning sign said "Those with epilepsy are advised not to participate"). The days passed with me just watching my life, and I felt unnoticed and unheard. To top it off, I didn't even have control over my own body because I was having seizures daily. There were only a few people who spoke to me or noticed me because of just one problem: I had Epilepsy.

I was so sick and tired of people feeling sorry for me. A person with a disability should never be treated differently or looked at differently just because of it. Everyone should be treated equally, regardless of their disabilities. People can feel it when you look down on them or treat them differently, and honestly, that truly hurts. I know it hurt me.

There is a good reason why people say, "Treat others as you would want to be treated." You should always present someone with a smile, even if they're not your favorite person. If you treat someone differently than others, they begin to feel degraded and looked down upon. While I was growing up and still to this day, kids who are in special education are my best friends.

So many are so kindhearted and deserve the world, just like anyone else. You can't judge a book by its cover. I have been around special education kids all my life, and believe they should not have a different designation from us; they are just like everyone else. Except, these kids see you for who you are without any judgment. I think more kids should behave like them, and then school would become a much healthier environment.

Kids at school constantly had little side jokes or comments that destroyed me and no one even noticed. Or if they did, I never knew it—because they certainly never defended me. Looking back, I wish someone had spoken up, even once, to say that what was happening wasn't okay. That simple act of kindness could have changed everything. Because of those experiences, I've made a promise to myself that I will never stay silent when I see someone being belittled or marginalized. I know what it feels like to be invisible, to have your pain dismissed, and your worth questioned. No one should ever have to feel that way. It takes courage to speak up, but silence only allows cruelty to grow. Now, I make it a point to be a voice for others—to defend, to uplift, and to remind people of their value when the world tries to make them forget. Those moments of hardship taught me empathy, compassion, and the importance of standing beside others. I may not be able to erase my own past, but I can make sure no one around me ever feels alone in theirs.

I still remember this one time in middle school where a girl was laughing as she asked if I had a seizure. I knew she was making fun of my disability because she said "seizure" completely wrong, saying "sheishure" mockingly ,and then also acted out a seizure in her chair. I just diverted her attention, but never answered her because I was too embarrassed and hurt to be transparent about it.

Never Give Up

Hard times may be exhausting, but they shape us into who we are meant to become. Without challenges, our lives would look completely different—we wouldn't have the strength, wisdom, or resilience we carry now. Life is like the weather— you never truly know what's coming next. When it feels as though everything is falling apart, that's often the moment you're being called to keep pushing forward. Life isn't meant to be easy; it's meant to be possible. The hardships I've faced have helped me develop emotional intelligence at a young age— to remain calm in the midst of chaos, to trust in the Lord, and to keep Him at the center of my life and relationships. Where there is difficulty, there may also be divine purpose—sometimes, God allows challenges not to break us, but to test and strengthen our faith.

1 Peter 1:7 "Your faith will be like gold that has been tested in a fire. And these trials will prove that your faith is worth much more than gold that can be destroyed. They will show that you will be given praise and honor and glory when Jesus Christ returns."

You can't give up!

You have two choices in life: you can either give up or persevere through all the hardship you face. God never said it would be easy, but it is possible, and all of your hard hard work will be rewarded. If I gave up, I would not be where

I am today- as long as you believe miracles do happen.

Epilepsy is starting to become more common as the years pass, and it's important to know what to do if someone were to have a seizure. If you are ever around someone who is experiencing a seizure here are my personal tips to properly help:

1.) as they fall keep them close to your body and protect their head always

2.) place them on their side to avoid aspiration

3.) make sure the surroundings are safe and there is nothing that could   cause injury to the person

4.) stay with them throughout the entirety of the seizure and make sure they are okay

5.) not a requirement but it always helps to pray for healing throughout every difficulty. Psalm 41:1 says: "God is our refuge and strength, a very present help in trouble."

If you know anyone who has epilepsy and you're not sure how to react in the correct way, stay calm and support the head of the person experiencing the seizure. Do your best to help them avoid injury.

I believe you should not give up during difficult times. You learn and become better by persevering through hard times. God doesn't expect us to endure by our own strength. He promises renewed strength to those who lean on Him. When we feel like giving up, He is our source of power and endurance.

Isaiah 40:31 "But they that wait upon the LORD shall renew their strength; they shall mount up with wings as eagles; they shall run, and not be weary; and they shall walk, and not faint."

Chapter 2: Waves of Silence

When I was three years old, and my sister, Lindsay, was seven years old, my parents got a divorce. I was extremely confused given I was only three, and I wasn't able to comprehend what was going on or know how to handle it. The first time we went to see my dad after the divorce was terrifying to me! He felt like a stranger. I was only four years old, looking back out of his car window for my mom. When I didn't see her anymore, I began to break down in tears. I would cry and cry until Lindsay would hug me tight and tell me, "Everything will be okay!" Lindsay is my best friend and has always known how to comfort me and make me smile. Every time Lindsay and I went to go see our Dad, it would get less terrifying.

I would always be extra cautious about my seizures when we would visit Dad because it seemed he just didn't understand or even try to understand. My dad would often keep walking as I was having a seizure and rarely look back. Maybe he felt uncomfortable or had a hard time watching his baby girl like that. But whatever it was, he seemed to pay little attention to them.

Once while we were on a bike ride, I told both my sister and dad that I had to sit down because I was about to have a seizure. The only option was to lie down on private property because the only other choice was the road. My sister stopped and sat with me, making sure my head was supported. My dad was still going on his bike and after a while, he eventually turned around noticing neither of us were with him. He never even got off his bike to make sure I was okay. This was one reason I was always extra worried about my seizures while I was with him. I remember trying to stay by Lindsay's side just in case I was to have one; I knew she would be there for me. When I went to Jacksonville, Lindsay was like my baby blanket; she was by my side through all my struggles.

Out of all my family members, other than my mom, I believe my sister understood my seizures the best and how to react to them as well. She always knew exactly what to say and when to say it. She was always there when I needed her, and she would sit with me. Sometimes she would hold me if she was scared I would get hurt while having a seizure. She spoke with intention, not just flowing thoughts. Lindsay never looked at me differently from the others, which made me feel like an equal. She is my true built-in best friend and has been there for me all my life.

After a year of living in Albany, I met my best friend, Jacquelyn Hawkins, at the age of four. Jacquelyn and I met in a dance class at Pritchett Pippin, but when we met, she would act like a dog in class. Jacquelyn was the type of kid to run on all fours. I even remember eating and drinking out of bowls like a dog when I went to her house for one of the first times. We were convinced that we were dogs at one point. Even though I didn't talk much back then, she figured maybe I was deaf. She was determined to make me her friend, and I'm so glad it worked. I had no clue that she and I would become lifelong friends. Jacquelyn became like a sister to me after all the years of friendship. She knows me better than anyone else, and she has stayed by my side through all the bumps along the road of life. I remember Jacquelyn and her mom used to pray healing prayers with me. They helped bring me closer to God at such a young age, and she is one of the reasons I was able to continue having a good relationship with God throughout my life. We would go to church together and talk about the word of

God and what big plans he has in store for us in the future.

Grace In My Weakness

During Bible study at church one time, I felt an aura, which is the feeling I get right before I have a seizure. The feeling eventually went away, and I felt myself falling out of my chair, but I had no control over what was happening. I was experiencing a grand mal seizure. I blacked out and was unconscious for approximately five minutes. The church tried to call the ambulance, but Jacquelyn told them not to. Jacquelyn quickly ran down the hall to her mom's Bible study, grabbed her, and they both ran to me. I eventually woke up, not knowing what had happened. I had hit my head and had a bruised chin. After that, they took me home to rest because having a seizure can make you extremely tired, especially grand mals. It is just all your muscles working simultaneously, like a muscle spasm. That gets tiring when all your muscles have been at work!

Before I got out of the car when they dropped me off at my house, we said a prayer: "Dear Lord, take these seizures away, keep her safe, and guide her to your healing, Amen."

When I got home I remember my mom rushing to the door with worry written all across her face. She said " Honey, are you okay?" and gave me a hug. I hugged my mom for a while because I felt safe in her arms after a rough morning. She always knew how to comfort me and remind me that everything was going to be okay. I remember crying from the overwhelming amount of emotion I was experiencing. I used to wonder what it was like not to have seizures and to not to have to worry about what I would do if one happened.

When I had seizures, I felt embarrassed or ashamed. Shame is a powerful emotion that occurs when you believe something is fundamentally wrong with you. It is a highly unpleasant and isolating experience caused by feelings of unworthiness, inadequacy, or humiliation. Shame can appear as a heavy load that drags us down as we go through life, making us feel inadequate and unworthy of love and acceptance. Overcoming this takes patience and self-acceptance. I overcame these difficulties by turning to the Lord not only during bad times but the good times as well. Also by expressing my feelings and shame, I learned over the years the negative things that can happen when you try to bottle up all your emotions. It's okay to not be okay. God is always there for you! I overcame these feelings of shame by turning to the Lord not only during the bad times but the good times as well. By doing this it showed me the positive aspects from not bottling up all your emotions.

Throughout my life, no one liked seeing me in pain, but all they could do was wait for the seizure to be over. Maybe it was because I was embarrassed or ashamed, but when I would have a seizure, I would tend to push the people I love away so they wouldn't see me in pain. I could see the sadness in their eyes when they would watch me seize as they tried to understand what I was going through. Having a seizure disorder made a giant impact on my life and my family's lives. I could see in people's eyes surrounding me that they felt sorry for me, but I never understood why they felt such sadness towards me. One of the ways I was treated differently was even those I loved put limitations on me to help keep me safe. It hurt a lot and even though I couldn't completely understand their sorrow towards me, maybe the truth was I felt sorry for myself too. At the time it was difficult for me to understand why I couldn't do what others did. For example, I was unable to stay up late with friends. While others could enjoy late-night conversations, sleepovers, or spontaneous plans, I often had to leave early or miss out altogether because a lack of sleep could trigger a seizure. Even when I wanted to push past the limits and feel "normal," my health had to come first, reminding me that my condition requires constant awareness and responsibility.

Chapter 3: Becoming Stronger

Growing up, I always knew I was different from others. I remember vividly one time in my grandma Meme's car when I was having a seizure. All I could wonder was why God made this my struggle. It seemed as if I kept getting thrown obstacles, and it felt like I was emotionally drowning. I still turned to God for comfort because I always knew he would heal me from my wounds when the time was right. "But I will restore you to health and heal your wounds, declares the LORD" (Jeremiah 30:17).

Life is already hard as it is, and having to deal with this issue daily tore my heart to pieces. I constantly reminded myself that I wouldn't have seizures for the rest of my life. I had hope for my restoration and believed that something good was coming. God is our al-mighty comforter!

Waking up every morning just to have a seizure made me feel numb to the point where I didn't even want to go to school anymore. The opening of my eyes caused a sudden stimulus to run through my brain, causing an electrical imbalance which led to a seizure each time. I would have a seizure in the middle of the night sometimes, even if I barely opened my eyes. The seizures in the middle of the night were some of my worst. My whole body would jerk uncontrollably and I would nearly fall off my bed. At times I had to drag my leg up to my chest so that when my leg jerked it would go back down. But I could not move my leg at all by myself, so as I pulled it toward me it felt like an extremely heavy weight. The seizures would make me feel very exhausted after the constant muscle contractions.

I saw school as hell because every time I would have a seizure people would look down on me or even laugh at me as if I were a joke. Then, I couldn't even defend myself because the high emotion could trigger a seizure. I couldn't ever say or be who I actually was or show how I felt. I felt weak - as if I could do nothing. Everything felt out of control, as I got lost in this time of tragedy that seemed never-ending.

I never complained during this battle, even while facing such hardship. I always kept the perspective that someone else out there may be carrying a heavier burden, which helped me remain grounded. Instead of focusing on what I was going through, I leaned into prayer and opened up to my best friend, Jacquelyn. She is someone I am incredibly grateful for and a person God clearly placed in my life when I needed her most. Growing up, if I had allowed my seizures to defeat me and dictate my happiness, I would be a completely different person today. Choosing to fight for my joy rather than surrender to my circumstances shaped who I am. When you truly fight for what you want, there is a strong chance it will come to fruition and be worth every ounce of effort you put into it.

Once you experience a traumatic battle in your life, you begin to look at things differently. When it comes to conversation, there are some things you just cannot say because you never know what battle someone may be facing. My advice to you is to watch what you say because words can cut deeper than a knife. As it says in Proverbs 12:18, "The words of the reckless, pierce like swords, but the tongue of the wise brings healing."

Always think before speaking because words can have an extreme amount of impact on a person. Someone once said to me while I was having a seizure, "Why are you having a seizure?" It felt like they thought my seizures were my fault which was extremely untrue- I did nothing to cause my seizures they just were. I did not want to have a seizure at any point in my life but it was part of me and it made me strong as an individual. This comment actually taught me to be tough and to not care what others said as long as I know the truth.

Through all of the words I endured, I became more aware of the power of words and the impact words can have on others. I strive to use my words to lift others up and not tear them down.

My Fight Song

The song "Control" by Zoe Wees is actually about fighting through epilepsy. Although her exact diagnosis was different from mine, it was a song that I could listen to and feel completely understood. It has so much truth to it- I didn't want to lose control but there was nothing I could do about it. Sometimes even now I think it's coming but I know it's not.

Another song I would listen to when life would try to knock me down was the song "Titanium." Most times I would have a seizure, and then I would listen to that song afterward. There was one verse repeated in the song that always stuck out to me: "You shoot me down, but I won't fall; I am titanium." This was my fight song.

If you set your mind to the fact that you are strong and cannot be stopped, you are capable of anything. Everyone is a warrior, they just might be in different battles. No one may fully understand the battles another person may face because they have not experienced them. Every person may view you differently, but no matter how they view you, it really only matters how you view yourself. How you view yourself (and by extension how you treat yourself) is the most important perspective a person could have. Self-love is key to a truly happy life, because you can't be happy if you are not happy with who you are. Music helped me to encourage myself and see myself as strong and capable, even when I wasn't feeling like it.

As it explains in the scripture Matthew 22:37-39 "Jesus said unto him, Thou shalt love the Lord thy God with all thy heart, and with all thy soul, and with all thy mind. This is the first and great commandment. And the second is like unto it, Thou shalt love thy neighbour as thyself" (KJV). This verse shows healthy self-love — "as thyself" — as the standard by which we love others. You cannot love others well if you do not first understand your own God-given value and love yourself in a way that honors God.

When a person feels like they're constantly being torn down, self-love can be hard sometimes. As it is written in Song of Solomon 4:7, "You are altogether beautiful, my darling" (NASB). God sees you as altogether beautiful and He loves you so much. Everyone has flaws, but you should embrace them rather than hide them. Your flaws and background are what make you, you. Growing up, all I saw were my flaws and what was wrong with me, rather than the good parts about myself. I spent so much of my life tearing myself down rather than building myself up, so I would turn to God and ask for His help when I was at my lowest. Many people may think praying is a waste of time, but I believe that, over time, your prayers will be answered. You just have to be patient. God hears our prayers even when they are not answered in our timing; they will be answered in His timing.

Throughout school, I often felt like a shadow — present, but unseen, as if I didn't have a voice. I remember saying once that I felt like I didn't have a life, and in many ways, that's exactly how it felt. A shadow isn't something real or tangible; it exists, but it's not truly there. That's how I felt — existing, but not really living. In elementary school, kids used to laugh at me because I was different. Remember, some would even pretend to have seizures in their chairs just to mock me, making me feel more ashamed and isolated than I already did. I was constantly reminded that I wasn't viewed the same as everyone else.

Even though their words hurt deeply, I never let anyone see how much it affected me. I told myself that life was too short to care about what others thought. So instead, I held in my feelings, but I didn't keep them there- I prayed about them! I often asked God why my life had to be so different and why I had to face challenges that others didn't seem to understand. Over time, I learned to grow from that pain instead of letting it break me. I discovered that if you are happy with who you are, that's what truly matters.

Life can feel like standing in the middle of a storm without an umbrella — exposed, vulnerable, and unsure where to turn. I've been there too. But through those moments, I found something special: strength. I learned to be content with myself, to trust in God, and to stay strong in the face of adversity.

I Didn't Have to Be Alone

One of my biggest seizures I remember was in fourth grade. We lined up in the cafeteria as we were about to leave to walk back to the classroom and I began to feel an aura. Within that minute I sat down and began to seize over and over again as I was fully conscious. The principal and nurse came with a wheelchair. To ensure that I was okay, they wheeled me down to the nurse's office. After the nurse asked me a few questions I was released to go back to class. As I was about to enter the classroom my stomach dropped from embarrassment. The room was filled with stares and questions as soon as I walked in. As they stared at me and I sank into my seat, I kept to myself. The teacher continued her lecture after the class settled.

There are times that you just need days to yourself because of the feeling of being overwhelmed, and that's okay. Life is hard and full of challenges, and my question to you is: How do you deal with your hardships?

Remember to always let your loved ones know what's going on because they are the people in your life who won't leave your side and will never judge you. Maybe it won't be the family you were born into. Family doesn't always have to be blood; it's about how they understand you, the feeling of being loved, and being there when you feel lost.

Throughout my hardships as a kid, I kept it all bottled inside, and although I gave it to God in prayer, I wish I had spoken to a family member about it too. Keeping it locked up has negative effects in the long run. All that pain, all that shame, I tried to deal with on my own. Yes, I talked to God, I prayed. But now I realize He gives us people for a reason. I had a support system right there, but I just didn't know how to reach out.

I should have trusted someone to open up to, and I should have asked for help. I should have leaned on my family for support. I should have realized that "family," those that are around you and understand you, will be there for you, no matter what. Now that I am older I know that they wanted to help, they wanted to listen and be there for me, but I didn't always let them.

Chapter 4: Hardships

My seizures became severely worse and more frequent during middle school and early high school. Kids in middle school didn't understand. Like that one girl who mocked me, they would mispronounce the word "seizure" and start laughing, thinking it was funny, even while I was actively having a seizure. That hurt and cut me deep but I kept going and kept my chin up. I knew God had greater plans for me. I wasn't going through this battle without some kind of light at the end of the tunnel. All that I went through made me mature very fast. I became very independent and strong-minded.

In middle school, I would ride the transfer bus every afternoon to the school my mom worked at, Lee County Elementary School. One of those afternoons I had a grand mal seizure on the bus. I was sitting on the right side of the bus and as we were getting dropped off at my mom's school I knew I didn't feel good. A guy told me I could go first off the bus, but when he stopped and let me go first, I said "No, you can go, I don't feel so good."

However, he insisted and since I was trying to hide my epilepsy, I got up and started walking down the aisle. I felt super dizzy, but I just kept thinking "this aura may just go away" because it felt weaker than normal. Within a minute of standing up and walking, I passed out and fell. I fell into the seat, and hit my face straight on the metal lining of the seats. I can't really explain how I felt in the moment given that I was unconscious but I can tell you how I felt before. I was scared; this aura felt different than normal. I knew something wasn't right. When I got up I was so nervous with all the worries about this aura rushing through my brain. Then a few seconds later I blacked out and I am unable to recall anything from during the seizure.

This seizure was caused by overheating. It was eighty degrees outside and I had on an undershirt, a hoodie, and jeans. They instantly called my mom to the bus ramp. She ran quickly down the hall to the bus. She frantically started taking off my coat. The school had also called 911, but she told them to tell them not to come because seizures were a normal thing for us. The only thing I truly remember is waking up in my mom's car not knowing what had happened. I asked her what happened and she responded upsettingly "You had a grand mal seizure, honey, and we're headed home. You need to get some rest."

Later that day, we went to eat at my grandparent's house for supper, and by that time both of my eyes were swollen and purple from the fall. Midway through supper my grandpa told me to come here and started to touch my cheeks and asked if it hurt and I responded with "Yes, that hurts a little bit." He told my mom to take me to the emergency room to make sure that I didn't seriously hurt myself. He told me I could have possibly fractured my cheekbone.

We went to the ER and waited for hours. When we finally got to see the doctor and do some X-rays he said nothing was broken, but not to put pressure on my cheeks since they are significantly swollen. We got home that night close to 12:30 in the morning and neither of us went to school the next day. I missed close to a whole week of school after that because of my face. I was also exhausted from such a large and long seizure. I kept asking my mom just one more day, then I'd go back to school. I didn't want to go back to school because I was scared of the comments I was going to get from my peers.

When I got back to school everyone kept asking questions about what happened, and I just dodged the questions because I felt too embarrassed to answer. I didn't talk much and just kept to myself because many of my peers taunted me saying I was not normal. I felt as if I wasn't seen as an equal to anyone. I just prayed each night that everything would be okay.

Isaiah 41:10, "Don't be afraid, For I am with you. Don't be discouraged, For I am your God. I will strengthen and help you. I will uphold you with my righteous right hand."

Hard Work Through Hard Days

Anytime there was a fire drill at school it would cause a seizure. I remember one time I felt an aura during a fire drill, but once again I didn't sit down because I thought it might go away. Immediately I fell to the concrete and got scraped up pretty badly. My IEP teacher stood next to me and waited for my seizure to be over. After getting up, I joined the other kids and just acted like everything was fine. Everything wasn't fine. Again, at that moment I felt so alone. I was tired of being different. Tired of not know-ing when my next seizure might hit, and I could be injured once again.

I got a phone at the beginning of middle school in case I had a seizure. For some reason, the teachers and principals would freak out, even though it was "no big deal." After all, it happened every day, multiple times a day. They would call my mom each time I had a seizure, asking what they should do to stop the seizure and why it was happening. My mom would always answer the same way, saying, "There's nothing you can do, but make sure she's safe." Things like that made me feel like I didn't have a voice. Like I was just standing there watching and nothing was within my control. I can't remember ever being asked what I wanted and what I believed would truly benefit the situation or "episodes," as my grandma used to call them.

In school, I used to occasionally feel stupid. I thought I wasn't learning anything. Given that I have seizures frequently—nearly six times a day—when people would speak to me while I was having one, I wasn't able to understand what they were saying, or I'd forget it right away, even if I had understood them. When having an episode or seizure, it can be very challenging to grasp information due to the im-balanced electrical current running through the brain. I was frustrated because I wanted to learn and participate in class, but my seizures made it difficult to keep up with the teachings. Because of their frequency, it was challenging for me to always understand and process what was being taught. I have always been a very hard worker and put my ALL into everything I do. I was not lazy. But, it was hard for me to stay motivated and stay on track with my goals, however I was determined to make it work.

Proverbs 13:4 states, "Lazy people want much but get little, but those who work hard will prosper."

I kept pushing myself and worked harder to reach success. I feel like because I worked hard I was able to succeed and accomplish goals in academics that I never would have if I had just given up. I always kept in the back of my head-that though my situation was difficult, there were so many other diseases and situations that could have been much worse than my own.

This life was never meant to be easy, because God never intended it to be. You are meant to be molded into the person you were meant to be by facing challenges. The journey of life is difficult, but it is worth it. With every passing day, I am seeing the results of my hard work and dedication. I aim to inspire others to never give up on their goals.

I had several goals. Ever since I was a little girl I had faith that God would take my seizures away. I wanted independence. I wanted to drive one day. I wanted to have the life that most teenagers have. I felt like I was always bubble-wrapped for fear of something happening to me. Like the time we went hiking out west and I was not allowed to go to the edge to see the scenery. It highlighted my disability and I felt like I was different from everyone else who got to experience the view. I know my mom had my best interest at heart, but it was still hard to feel like I could not do what most others could.

Luke 18:1, "One day Jesus told his disciples a story to show that they should always pray and never give up."

We can always turn to God for help and guidance. He will never leave us or forsake us. He will give us the strength and courage to continue no matter our circumstance or situation.

Chapter 5: Feeling of Emptiness

One of the worst seizures I had was in the eighth grade. We were on our way back from mass because, at the time, I went to a private Catholic school. (I changed schools again before my sophomore year of high school). On the walk back across the street from the church to St. Teresa's Catholic School, I didn't feel the seizure coming and fell to the ground, conscious and scared. The skin on the palm of my left hand had been scraped off from the concrete. I wiggled my way to the grass and sat alone until the seizure ended. No one helped me. My hand was gushing blood, and right after my seizure, I went straight to the bathroom and wrapped my hand in toilet paper. I was too ashamed to go to the nurse because I always felt embarrassed or judged, so I tried to handle the situations on my own. I had so many thoughts rushing through my head at a million miles per hour. My first thought was "How am I going to hide this scrape from everyone all day?" and then "How am I going to tell my mom about my fall?" Throughout the day my hand was constantly stinging since I never went to the nurse.

I just waited for the pain to fade.

Later that day, there was a math problem the teacher was discussing in class, and she asked me to come to the board and solve it. I came to the board to solve the equation, but the smart board was acting up. My teacher grabbed my hand as her acrylic nails dug into my raw skin from the fall. I clinched my opposite hand into a fist as a reaction to the pain. I wanted to scream inside because it hurt so badly, but I didn't; I just smiled and acted like everything was okay. The board eventually was fixed, and I solved the equation (yay!). Then she gave me a high five, which also hurt, but was not as bad. Right as I got back to my desk, I rewrapped my hand with tissues because I had nothing else to cover my hand with. I then held my hand tight to my chest as it stung from not being cleaned.

When I got home later that afternoon I put some Neosporin on it and didn't tell my mom until later that evening. When I first showed her she was like "Oh, it's just a little scrape," but she couldn't see it clearly because the lights were dimmed in the den. When I turned on the lights and showed her again, she did her "mom thing" and freaked out. She asked what hap-pened, cleaned it, put a bandaid on it, and also made me put ice on it because my palm was a little swollen from the fall.

A few days later, the scrape began to dry and kind of looked like a heart. Which I thought was pretty cool. Even after a painful fall, I was able to see a heart. I always saw the best in things or looked for the good rather than looking on the bad side. In every bad situation I would try to focus on the good. Like the time I had a seizure in the parking deck… yes, it was gross that I had to lay on the ground. But I was safe, not injured, and I was supported and surrounded by family.

Also, during a soccer game later that same year, I had a seizure. In the middle of the game, I felt an aura and had to sit down. I was playing striker at the time. Everyone was screaming at me to get up but I couldn't. Then, I got hit in the face with the soccer ball while I was seizing. All I felt was stress and worry. A seizure is never fun and can be frightening at times. Everyone was worried and confused about what was going on. My mom ran up to the sidelines to get me and waited with me until my seizure ended. Eventually, I was able to walk off the field and take a moment to feel at ease.

During this time in my life, I was having five to six seizures a day, and none were small either.

I had a seizure at school every day, but most of the time I was able to hide it. When they began to get worse, it made it even more difficult to hide my seizures. I felt so alone and like no one could hear me. But I never went a day without smiling, even if my day had been very challenging.

The year of ninth grade I broke my nose twice. The first time I broke my nose, I was in the bathroom. I sat down on the toilet and held onto the handicap bars to keep myself supported. Holding on to the bars wasn't enough though. The jerking of my body became out of control, and I lost my grip which caused me to fall straight onto my face. My nose instantly started bleeding, but I finally got the bleeding under control and went on about my day. I really just took toilet paper and tried to stop the bleeding and hid out in the bathroom until it stopped. I did not want others to know or worry about me. I didn't tell my mom about it because I didn't want to make her sad by seeing me hurt.

The next day, my mom saw my nose, and it had turned purple. So, she asked what happened and I finally told her. She got upset that I didn't tell her after it happened. The side of my nasal bone was out of place, but it was too late to get it fixed. I probably should have told my mom sooner, but now I have a little souvenir from that particular fall. I don't have any regrets with how I dealt with the seizure.

The second time I broke my nose was in my biology class. I felt the aura, so I held on tightly to my desk, but the jerking of my body became out of my control and I fell out of my desk straight on my face in the middle of class. My teacher ran to me and called in another teacher for help. They both placed me back at my desk when he should have just supported my head and left me on the ground. By placing me back in my chair, I then fell on my nose for the second time causing a bad rug burn and another nose bleed. He was frantic and unsure of what to do, but I couldn't speak because of my seizure restricting my verbal abilities. I literally could not talk even if I wanted to. My brain was on, my speech was not.

I felt very embarrassed as the whole class was staring at me after my seizure had gone away. I sank into my chair as my teacher redirected the class's attention to his lecture. People were asking me what had happened, but I felt so ashamed for being different that I just repeatedly dodged the question. My normal response was just to deflect the attention back onto them by asking about their day or how they were. My teacher talked to me after class, asking what he could have done better to prevent my second fall. I told him that if it were to happen again, they should support my head and leave me on the leveled ground to decrease the chances of falling.

Later that week was picture day for the yearbook. What great timing. My nose was still bruised, stained with deep shades of purple and blue from the falls I had endured earlier in the week. I tried to cover the marks with makeup, but no amount of concealer could hide the evidence of what I had been through. When the yearbook photos came back, I stared at them and felt overwhelmed. As a tear rolled down my face, every memory of the pain and each fall flooded back. Without hesitation, I walked to the nearest trash can and threw the pictures away. They were a reminder of a chapter in my life that I did not want to relive or carry with me.

Each day, I worked relentlessly to ensure that my disability did not control my life—or my mindset. I reminded myself that happiness is a choice: you can either focus on the hardships or intentionally seek out the good, even when it feels difficult. "You are stronger than you think you are" became my mantra. Holding onto those words helped me stand tall and refuse to be defined by what tried to knock me down.

No matter how many times I was pushed back, I chose to rise again—stronger each time. That resilience is something I will carry with me for the rest of my life.

Through it all, God was guiding and protecting me, reminding me not to give up when things felt unbearable. Yes, there were moments when life felt unfair and overwhelming—and those moments still arise from time to time—but they are part of life. Every setback teaches us something, and every struggle shapes us into stronger versions of ourselves. We grow through adversity, and each time we rise, we do so with greater strength and deeper faith.

The Battle Within Me

I was determined to make a better life for myself and to find strength within. I kept reminding myself that I was capable of overcoming any obstacle and that I could do anything I set my mind to. I was constantly motivating myself to live a life full of joy and positivity. Your battles don't define who you are, they shape you into the person you were meant to become. My battle was my constant seizing. And I was fighting for them to not define who I was.

Almost every day in gym class I would have a seizure, but I would hide it by just running to the restroom. I would sit in the stall or sometimes even have to lie on the ground to decrease the risk of falling. I would lie there until the seizure was over. The jerking of the seizure was so strong that if I wasn't on a flat leveled surface, just like in biology that one day, I would fall out of a chair or anything that didn't have complete support for my entire body.

The same year my doctor had informed me that I was in the twenty-fifth percentile of epilepsy patients that cannot be healed and that my seizures would never go away. Doctors thought my seizures were permanent. I already felt like a shadow. I could not envision the rest of my life in this constant state of fear or panic or "what if." So, I did the only thing I knew how to do. I prayed.... I prayed all day, every day, asking for healing.

Healing prayer:

"In the name of Jesus Christ, I am healed. I am healed by his love and faith and by my love and faith in Him. I love you Lord and in your name I am healed, Amen."

When doubt creeps into your healing journey, pause and offer a simple prayer, trusting that God hears you. His answers may not come immediately, but they will arrive at the exact moment they are meant to. When you believe that, with Him, you are never alone or unprotected, you begin to find peace even in uncertainty. There are times when healing does not look the way we hope or expect. Sometimes, the deepest form of healing is God calling someone home, allowing them to finally rest after a long and courageous fight. I believe God desires healing for everyone—not always in the way we want, but in the way He knows is best for our lives and our souls.

Chapter 6: Family is Everything

Throughout my entire life, my family has been there for me every step of the way. I would not be where I am today, or writing this book, without the people I love right by my side. Out of everyone in my life, I can, by far, say that my mom was there for me throughout every battle I faced. She has been my one constant. After passing out on the bus from my grand mal seizure, it was her car that I woke up securely in. She was the one driving me to the hospital to make sure there were no serious injuries. She was the person who came running to me every time she got notified I had a seizure at school. She was there for me no matter what the circumstances were.

During times of difficulty, I tended to push her away, but no matter what, she wouldn't leave my side. She constantly showered me with love and reminded me that I was not alone. I am blessed to have my mom as a mom. God knew she was meant to be a mom and had the unconditional love to share with her kids and many more. She is a constant light. There were times I didn't want to tell her about the seizures I had because I didn't want to make her upset. Every time I had one, I could feel the sadness that she was experiencing. There was a weight lifted off of my chest once I was healed, but there was also a weight lifted off of my mom's chest. I could tell that my mom felt the freedom too when I stopped having seizures.

> *Galatians 5:13 says, "For you were called to freedom, brothers. Only do not use your freedom as an opportunity for the flesh, but through love serve one another."*

This verse spoke to me because it highlights that we should fully trust and rely on the Lord, for he has a plan for all of us. He is always there for us throughout everything. After being healed I finally felt free. For years I felt trapped by my many limitations due to seizures. Once I stopped having them, something in me sparked. I could finally be my true loud and silly self without the worry of a seizure occurring. I became full of life and even stronger in my faith as I grew as an individual. Now I am a person full of vitality. I even went skydiving in 2023 for the very first time and loved every minute of it! I plan to go again soon! Going through life with epilepsy really made me appreciate my health once the Lord healed me.

My Circle of Faith

Along with my mom, my grandpa and grandma also supported me and played an important role in my life. My grandpa was very knowledgeable about my epilepsy and always knew what to do. He was a doctor for 45 years and always kept God at the center of everything. He guided me in faith and reminded me that in God's time, I would be healed. He always led me closer to God and to trust in what the Lord has in store for me. He told me that God does grant miracles as long as you believe and keep your faith in Him. Even if it does not happen when you want it to. Miracles do happen, you just have to have faith.

When my grandma would pick me up from school after a seizure, all I wanted to do was go home. She would play card games with me and we would drink coffee together at her house. I enjoyed our time, and we would even get Pa to play games with us. She helped me to continue to stay strong in my faith. She helped me to focus on the positive in life and know that things happen for a reason. In her journal, she even expressed how she was proud of me for always keeping the faith that God would heal me one day. Experiencing epilepsy and going through this daily made me into the person I am to-day.

My sister, also, was right by my side when I would experience a seizure outside of school. Lindsay always made me laugh, and helped me to have a positive perspective on the situation. When Lindsay and I had sleepovers when I was younger and I had a seizure, she would hold me tight and reassure me that everything would be okay.

She was my constant reminder to never lose faith. God shines through her each and every day. She has been there for me throughout all of my life and is my built-in best friend. She was my first dance partner, my partner in crime, and the one who always made me feel like I had a voice. Your outlook on the challenges in life can change everything. She helped me to keep a positive outlook on life by the way she supported me and understood my seizures. She always made sure I was okay and I am forever thankful for her.

Lindsay and me back in 2003. She is the best big sister.

My mom is my best friend. This was Mom and me back in 2007

Faith, Hope, and Love

As I've mentioned before, school was hard for me. I was constantly worried about my next seizure. It didn't help that every time I had a seizure, my mom would get notified and have to come to the school, and they would ask her, "What can we do to prevent her seizures from happening?" My mom would always respond saying, "There's nothing you can do. All you can do is ensure the support of her head and prevent any injuries." It had to have been difficult for her to feel helpless in those situations. But, she always did everything she could.

Life isn't always how we think it will be, but it's about how we react to the challenges we face. Everyone goes through challenges. Your battles are what make you, you. Even at times, when you feel completely and utterly alone, God is always with you!

Isaiah 43:2 tells us that God says "When you go through deep waters, I will be with you."

My relationship with Jesus helped me to feel comfortable in my own skin, even when I was living in a constant state of my body doing what I did not want it to do. Happiness does not equal being in control, but rather placing your trust in the one who made you. Family and friends help provide you with peace of mind and joy in your life; they should enhance your happiness. But, you will never be truly happy if you're not happy in your own skin. At the end of the day, nothing can fill the void of emptiness if you're not content with yourself. All the people you love and who love you just want to support you and be there for you in all that you do and experience.

1 Corinthians 13:13 says, "And now these three remain: faith, hope, and love. But the greatest of these is love."

Love, hope, and faith are very important aspects of life. All that you do should be done in love. Never lose your faith for God is always there for you. Remember to always tell and show the ones you love how much they truly mean to you. The people in my life always showed me how important I was, and because I had their love and support I was able to make it through even in the darkest of times. Life is short, so you must be intentional with everything you do and say.

Chapter 7: Never Stop Going

When I was fifteen years old, Dr. Garret, my neurologist at the time, referred me to Dr. Tatum, a neurologist at Mayo Clinic Hospital in Jacksonville, Florida. I had seen countless neurologists and none seemed to be of any help with my situation. My seizures kept progressively getting worse as time passed. I told my mom I wanted brain surgery. I was tired of the constant agony and repeated injuries from my seizures. In early June 2019, we had a consultation with Dr. Tatum because I was interested in the less invasive brain surgery they offered.

We talked for over an hour with Dr. Tatum discussing his questions and our answers. His questions were for example, "What medications have you tried?" or "Can you explain what the seizure feels like?" etc. Then he recorded himself talking extremely fast and documented everything we had said in the conversation within about five minutes. It was incredible! The less invasive surgery was called Laser Interstitial Thermal Therapy.

To determine if I was a candidate for the surgery, I would spend a week in the hospital. We scheduled an appointment for another EEG where they would connect electrodes to my head and chest to monitor my brain and seizure activity. My medication was gradually weaned down to cause a large convulsion so my doctors could pinpoint exactly where the interrupted electric current was in my brain. I ended up experiencing significantly more convulsions than expected. I ended up having four when they were only looking for one. I didn't remember any of them. When I experienced one seizure, I bit my tongue so badly that one side got swollen and discolored. I had been bed-bound that entire week. It was hard because I felt lost and like no one really understood what I was going through, but my mom was right by my side.

Within a couple of weeks to a month, we learned I was not eligible for surgery as a result of the location of my focal cortical dysplasia. Dr. Tatum found that the spot on my brain was located in the left temporal lobe which involved: personality, memory, emotion, movement, and auditory ability. It was a very tough time for me because I had just gone through all the seizures and a week-long stay at the hospital and I was not a candidate, but God had a better plan. I was not a candidate for the surgery because of the risks involved. If I did get the surgery, I would not be able to do what I was capable of doing before. I would not be who I am today if I had gone through with the surgery. I am thankful for all the people who stuck by my side throughout this journey. It was a hard week, and even harder to accept this was not my answer, my healing had not miraculously been found yet.

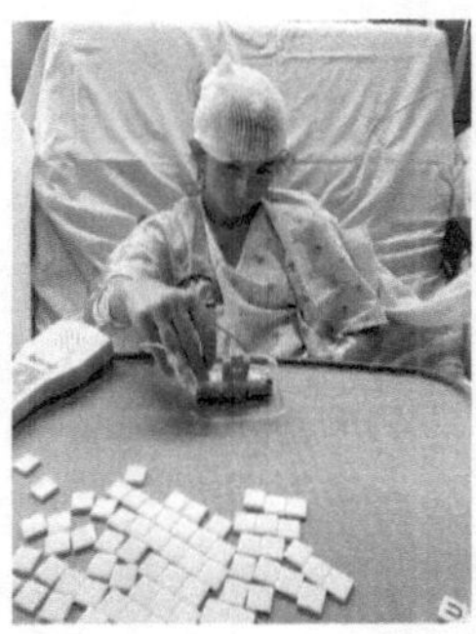

Stevie Lewis, 16 years old on June 24th, 2019.

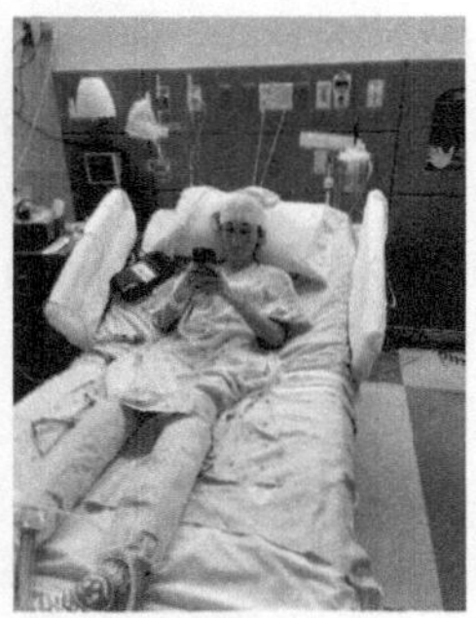

The leg compressions were to keep my blood regulated.

When we met with Dr. Tatum, he asked about the frequency, duration, and severity of my seizures. He also asked which medications I had tried. He then listed off different medications and there was one that I hadn't tried, Clobazam. Because I was not a candidate for surgery, I was sent home and was given a new prescription. All through the day, I prayed for these seizures to be taken away from me and for this lifelong battle to end. Being so limited in what I was able to do felt like I was being held back from reaching my full potential. Even though my mom and step-dad put limits on what I could do to avoid injury, sometimes I would do it anyway so as to not to feel so deprived of normal kid activities. I was always stubborn in that way.

Approximately two months after taking Clobazam, my seizures changed. Instead of my entire body jerking it was more like a sharp pain starting from my head on the way down to my right leg. I remember waking up and just instantly being in pain from the seizure. They did become less frequent, now at about two to three a day which was amazing. The doctors never thought I would be healed but I never stopped believing that God would heal me in His timing. My prayer was a constant one. My prayer was simple and direct. I prayed, "God, heal me when I am 16 years old because I want to be able to drive."

My family and I went to a Mexican restaurant on August 13th, 2019, to have supper and Bobby, my stepdad, drove me home early so I could work on my homework. Right after I got out of the car, as I was heading to the door, I felt an aura. I said, "Hey Bobby, I need to sit down for a second," and then I had a seizure in the grass. The seizure lasted approximately four minutes. It wasn't so much a jerking of my leg as a sharp pain.

August 13th was also my mom's cousin's birthday; she was actually the labor & delivery doctor the night I was born, which was special. That day, August 13th, 2019, became significant for another reason.

That was the day I had my last seizure.

I didn't know at the time that it would be my last. But then weeks passed. And then months. Finally, several months passed and I hadn't had a single seizure since that day. I was, as you might guess… 16 years old! And I was healed!

The Freedom I Dreamed Of

On March 20, 2020, two months before I turned seventeen, I received my driver's license. I was able to fulfill my lifelong dream of driving and gaining independence. I thank the Lord every day for healing me.

Mark 5:34 says, "He said to her, 'Daughter, your faith has made you well. Go in peace. Your suffering is over" (NLT). My faith had healed me. And I found myself in a place I had never truly been before, in peace.

A year later on August 13th, 2020, we celebrated the one year anniversary of me being healed. My beautiful-hearted mom and sister were there to celebrate my healing with me. This was a true miracle given to me by God. The doctors always said that I would have seizures forever, but little did they know what God had in store for me.

After being healed many of my family members told me that something in me had sparked. There was a weight lifted off of my chest, the weight of constant worry and stress about where to sit or what would happen to my body and if I would sustain yet another injury if I had a seizure. When I had seizures I was extremely shy and reserved; now if you ask people I don't ever shut up (in a positive way of course!). Now I am more extroverted and always down to go on an adventure. I believe that I am full of life and try to see the positive in every day. I have been told by many throughout my life that I glow in faith, but I know that's true because I experienced a miracle!

Chapter 8: Life After

In my sophomore year of high school I started school at Worth County High School. I played Soccer and my position was a striker for the team. That was also the first year I didn't experience a seizure on the Soccer field, which gave me a sense of security. My mind was finally free and I could finally do what I wanted to do without fear of serious injury. My favorite part of soccer was running. I've loved to run ever since I can remember. I used running as a sense of therapy for myself to ease the stresses of life.

Junior year of high school I participated in Soccer and Track & Field. In track, I ran the 800, 4x800, 1600, and 3200 meters. One of my favorite races was the 1600 because it pushed my limits and never got boring. I loved my sports and the sports family I gained through them. I had a strong relationship with my athletic trainer who was one of my biggest supporters and helped me to avoid injury. The fact that I was even able to be a part of a team, despite all its ups and downs, made me feel extremely blessed. Throughout it all, I would not be where I am without following the word of the Lord and having the people I love by my side. Throughout my life God has continually blessed me with such amazing people to be surrounded by. This journey would have looked completely different without the ones I love dearly.

Senior year of high school I was able to join Cross Country and that was by far my favorite sport I ever participated in. I then got the chance to compete at the state level for Cross Country. During the late spring, I competed in all four of my Track & Field events at state. During that same year, one of my best friends and I completed a certified nursing assistant (CNA) program together and received our CNA licenses. I enjoyed the classes that were included in the program. It contained many things that would contribute to my field of study in college and the future career I was seeking.

It provided great hands-on experience in the healthcare field. In May 2022, I graduated high school with honors and completed two pathways, both agriculture and the CNA program. I was selected for a scholarship toward college. It was an honor to be selected for such an honorable scholarship. At the end of graduation, my friend and I did our last secret handshake before I went off to college and doing it made my heart feel so full. It was a pleasure to be surrounded by such amazing and supportive family and friends. Graduating with a GPA of 3.8 with honors was amazing. Even my doctor was proud of my accomplishment because of the focal cortical dysplasia in my brain. I worked very hard to study and learn because I did have this dysplasia (a spot on my brain, where neurons did not disperse) that actually slowed down its processing. But I did not let that stop me.

That summer I worked four different jobs to try to save up some money for college in the Fall. Being healed from the seizures meant I could drive to all my jobs as I needed to, so I'm happy everything worked out as it did.

I worked as a lifeguard, waitress, bartender, and babysitter. My experience working as a lifeguard was enjoyable because I got to interact with so many people. I actually met the kids I babysat at the country club while lifeguarding. They were such sweet kids with big personalities. It was a joy to be a part of their lives. I even taught swimming lessons to a few kids, which positively impacted me just as much as them. I enjoyed all of my jobs, but it surely was a busy summer. I can hardly believe how quickly it flew by. Thankfully, I was able to save up a good amount of money for college.

I decided to go to Augusta University, which was my top choice school. I chose this college because it is great for an education in health-care, and I was planning on pursuing a career in that field. I chose Kinesiology, the study of the movement of the body, as my major because it truly fascinated me. It also aligned with my concentration in Pre-Occupational Therapy. I was a little bit of a nerd when it came to study-ing Kinesiology. I kept a good bit of my grand-pa's medical books, and when a topic would interest me I would look for it in the books to try and grasp a full understanding of the topic.

Growing up with seizures caused me to be extremely motivated in school, even if it was harder for me than others. I gave my all to my education and many of my teachers recognized that. I was that "annoying" kid in high school that would be upset by receiving a B on an as-signment. I just had very high expectations for myself, and wanted to become someone I was proud of. I knew that if I worked hard then it would pay off in the future, and it did.

I entered college as a Kinesiology major with a concentration in Occupational Therapy, but my connection to this profession began long before I ever stepped onto a college campus. During my senior year of high school, I had the opportunity to shadow at a hospital in my hometown. Watching occupational therapists work so intentionally with their patients—helping them regain independence, dignity, and confidence in their daily lives—deeply moved me. It was in those moments that I realized occupational therapy was more than a career; it was a way to truly serve others during some of their most vulnerable times. From that experience on, I felt a strong sense of purpose guiding me toward this path.

As a child, I once dreamed of enlisting in the Air Force, hoping to serve my country in uniform. When that dream was no longer possible due to my medical history, I struggled to understand why that door had closed. With time, faith, and reflection, I came to see that God had a different plan for me—one that still allowed me to serve those who serve our nation. My aspiration is to become a military occupational therapist, working with service members as they recover from injury and work to reclaim their independence, confidence, and sense of self. I hope to specialize in neuroscience, where I can help individuals heal not only physically, but emotionally and mentally as well. I believe our most challenging moments shape our deepest callings, and it is through those experiences that God prepares us for the purpose He has placed on our hearts.

My faith has guided me through many challenges, shaping me into someone who values resilience, compassion, and gratitude. During my freshman year of college, I joined the Center for Undergraduate Research and Scholarship (CURS), where I was selected to participate in a summer research program. My project focused on how dementia affects sleep, which taught me the importance of patience, communication, and evidence-based care. Presenting my research in front of peers and mentors, and later at the Gerontological Society of America National Research Conference in Tampa, Florida, was one of the most meaningful experiences of my academic journey. It deepened my respect for the aging population and reinforced my desire to make a tangible difference in people's lives.

After returning from the conference, I began working as a Physical Therapy Aide to gain more clinical experience. While I appreciated the field, I soon realized that occupational therapy truly aligned with my heart and purpose. Later, I transferred to the University of North Georgia for a fresh start, and it turned out to be one of the best decisions I have ever made. The mountains surrounding the campus, the supportive community, and the sense of peace I felt reminded me that I was exactly where I was meant to be. I began to see God's hand in every detail of my journey.

Now, I strive to live each day with intention and gratitude. I wake up early to write, reflect, and work on my goals. I've joined a CrossFit gym and train four times a week, which has strengthened not just my body but also my discipline and perseverance. I also volunteer at Chelsey Park Health & Rehabilitation three times a week, where I assist and observe occupational therapists. Every day spent with the residents reminds me why I chose this path—to give hope, to empower, and to help others find joy and independence again.

Through every challenge, I have learned that God's plan is greater than my own. Ephesians 3:20 says, "Now to him who is able to do far more abundantly than all that we ask or think, according to the power at work within us," (ESV) and I see that truth reflected in my journey every day. I am ready to serve, to learn, and to dedicate my life to helping others—especially the men and women who have sacrificed so much for our country. Occupational therapy is not just a career for me; it is a calling, and I am honored to follow it.

"Don't get discouraged by God's silence. He is working in ways that will surprise you." - Nicole Arbuckle

The above quote inspired me and also reminded me that God works in mysterious ways. God wants the best for us, always. You must trust in God's plan for you and lay it all on Him. During my time of hardship, I strongly felt that God was preparing me for something better. Every battle we face we learn and grow from it. Looking back now, I have grown significantly within this past year.

Battles do not define who you are, they sculpt you into who you were meant to be. Each person faces some type of battle throughout their lives, but how you respond to them is what matters most.

Chapter 9: Love

The most important thing in life is choosing to become love, even when you are dealt a bad hand. Becoming love means responding to pain with compassion instead of bitterness, and choosing grace when anger would be easier. It is deciding that hardship will not harden your heart, but instead deepen your empathy for others who are struggling. When life wounds you, becoming love is the act of refusing to let those wounds define you; instead, you allow them to shape you into someone more patient, understanding, and kind.

In difficult moments, you are faced with a choice: to draw closer to God or to turn away from Him. Becoming love is choosing to lean into faith when answers are unclear and trusting that God is working even in silence. It is loving deeply despite the risk of being hurt again, because love reflects God's presence in our lives. Through love, we forgive when it feels impossible, we show mercy when it is undeserved, and we remain hopeful when circumstances suggest otherwise.

To become love is not weakness—it is strength rooted in faith. It is waking up each day and deciding that no matter what you face, you will lead with compassion, humility, and trust in God's plan. When you choose love, you allow God to work through you, turning pain into purpose and trials into testimony.

1 Peter 4:8 states, "Above all, love each other deeply, because love covers over a multitude of sins" (NLT). People will disappoint you. There will be people that you dislike, but those are the ones that God truly wants you to share Christ-like love to. Many of my family members have taught and mentored me in a way that resembles Christ's love. My grandparents were great examples of people who express and show Christ-like love daily. Through my hard times they led me to prayer rather than resentment toward Christ.

Pray for the people in your life and even the ones you're not so fond of. Everyone is a child of God. Don't miss the opportunity to make someone's day by giving them a compliment or doing something kind for them. Your kind words can change someone's life. Nobody is perfect, and we have all hit rock bottom at some point in our lives, but it is the way we recover that matters. It is important to lean on God- for He is always with you and has your best interest at heart always. He will forgive you of all your sins.

1 John 1:9 says, "If we confess our sins, he is faithful and just to forgive us our sins and to cleanse us from all unrighteousness" (ESV).

Look back at how far you have come. Never go back, always move forward. When you fall, get back up and persevere through the difficult times. I know it may seem like God is silent, but He works in silence. He has a plan for you. Give His love to others and you will build a stronger and closer relationship with Him. Throughout the Bible this phrase is repeated: "Be not afraid."

As hard as it is, don't be afraid of the hard times and be reassured by God's presence in your life. As you're coming to the end of the book, look around and see all the good that is in your life. The things you do have are blessings, because life is not about what you don't have; it's about what you do have.

You are constantly growing as an individual, like a tree. Now, what does a tree have to do with this? Please bear with me. We begin as a seed, grow continuously during our lives, and eventually become a tree filled with beautiful leaves. Leaves can be shown as growth and characteristics that describe us. For example, a leaf could be a characteristic of discipline, honesty, loyalty, etc. We often think of blessings as things, but blessings can be those God given attributes that he "grows" in us on the journey of life. My close family and my best friend Jacquelyn have all been blessings in my life. Each of them were there for me every step of the way.

We are constantly growing and learning throughout our daily lives. Love also makes us grow, and God is love! When you show a tree some love by watering it, it grows, and we are the same way. Love gives us a sense of comfort and support, so even if we fail, we know everything will be okay. Without failure we would never grow. Life is one big lesson, so go out and give love to others so they can grow. To choose to love even when it's hard is a Christ-like love.

My journey of healing was definitely filled with ups and downs. I had good and bad days, but I always remembered it was part of the plan, "This too shall pass" in its own time. Having epilepsy did not keep me from giving out love to others. I was more reserved and nervous though, and so since my healing, I have been able to open up and share even more of the lessons that I have learned and the love that I have found in God.

After I stopped having seizures, both my cousin and my sister told me it was like night and day. I opened up and now I am more bubbly, outgoing, and sharing the Word of God with everyone. I want to make sure everyone is okay, even when I am not.

Love is all around you!

Chapter 10: Loved One's Point of View

From a mother's point of view, the time in my daughter's life when she experienced seizures was extremely difficult.

It started on an October morning around 9:30 a.m. I was in the kitchen with my five-month-old baby, Stevie Leigh Lewis. She was sitting on the counter in her baby seat while I prepared breakfast. I stepped away briefly to my room to grab my slippers, and when I returned, I saw my baby seizing for the very first time.

Her face was gray-blue. Her eyes were rolling back in her head, twitching. She was spitting up while her entire body jerked uncontrollably.

My heart dropped.

My sister's first child had seizures, so I imme-diately recognized what was happening—and I knew how serious it could be. I called 911 right away. When the ambulance arrived, they rushed us to the hospital. I couldn't stop staring at my baby, and I couldn't hold back my tears.

At the hospital, doctors quickly evaluated her and told us it was a febrile seizure, caused by a slight fever. They prescribed Trileptal and Phenobarbital.

But two weeks later, she had another seizure - this time without a fever.

My heart dropped all over again.

I called the doctor, and we went back to the hospital. That's when she was diagnosed with epilepsy.

Epilepsy is a neurological condition that affects the brain and causes recurrent, unprovoked seizures. It can affect people of all ages, races, and backgrounds. Later, we learned that Stevie had a spot on her left temporal lobe of her brain that was triggering the seizures.

From that point on, seizures became part of her everyday life. She would have several each day. We tried multiple medications, but nothing completely stopped them. Trileptal seemed to help the most, but the seizures never fully went away.

I worried constantly. Every single day, I prayed they would stop. It broke my heart every time I watched her go through one.

My dad, Dr. Edwin E. Flournoy, a family physician, told me to try not to make a big deal out of her seizures when they happened. He said this was part of her life, and I needed to stay calm for her. So every time she had a seizure, I focused on keeping her safe. On the outside, I stayed composed—but inside, my heart was breaking.

When Stevie was three years old, my mother and I traveled to Augusta, Georgia, to learn about a possible surgery. The doctors told us it had about a 70% chance of success, but a 30% chance of leaving her in a vegetative state.

It was an extremely invasive procedure. They would open her skull, allow her to have seizures while connected to EEG wires for several days, then remove the part of the brain where the seizures originated. Afterward, they would close her head, which would swell significantly during recovery. My dad and I had to make a decision that no one wants to ever have to face. In the end, we chose not to move forward with the surgery. I simply could not take that risk with my baby.

Augusta Georgia, 2006

Stevie grew up having seizures everywhere—at stores, in the car, at school, in parking lots, at malls in Atlanta, on walks, and even on bike rides. It became part of our everyday life. I worried constantly for her safety. I would often tell her, "I wish God would take these seizures away." Even at just seven years old, she would respond with such strong faith: "He will, Mom, in His own time." Sometimes she would even say, "He will when I am sixteen years old." As she got older, she began to feel an aura before a seizure.

Most of the time, she had just enough warning to sit down wherever she was—whether it was on a dirty Dollar Store floor, in a dark underground parking lot in Las Vegas, or while riding a bike with her dad in Jacksonville. No matter where she was, she would sit or lie down and let her body do what it did. Her legs would jerk, and then, just like that, she would get back up and keep going. I tried to be strong, but it was incredibly hard. I felt helpless. There was nothing I could do to make the seizures stop. There were days I thought it was so unfair. I would get angry and ask God, "Why her? She is so sweet, so brave, and so strong in her faith. Why won't you take this away?" I remember being at work teaching when the school would call to tell me she had another seizure. I would have to leave during my break or after school to attend a meeting with her teachers. Each time, I would explain there wasn't much we could do except keep her safe and wait for it to pass. Those calls broke my heart every single time.

For 16 years, my heart felt shattered. But I held onto Psalm 34:18: "The Lord is close to the brokenhearted; He rescues those whose spirits are crushed."

I remember one moment vividly—we were in the car, and Stevie had a seizure in the back seat. My mom gently held her hand and waited quietly for it to pass. I know she weas praying for strength in that moment. It happened at church almost every Sunday. If we were singing, one of us—my mom, my dad, Lindsay, or I—would sit with Stevie in the pew while everyone else stood. We stayed beside her until it passed.

A neurologist once told us Stevie was in the twenty-fifth percentile, meaning her seizures may never go away. We tried around nine different medications, but nothing completely worked. He suggested a neurostimulator implant—a device placed in the chest to help detect and stop seizures. But there were no guarantees, and given how small she was and the teasing she had already experienced, I didn't feel at peace with that decision.

So I asked about a second opinion. That's when we were referred to Dr. William Tatum at Mayo Clinic in Jacksonville, Florida. Dr. Tatum was incredible. He spent over an hour with us, then perfectly summarized everything we discussed. He prescribed another medication called Clobazam, which was one we had never tried before. He also recommended a video EEG to see if she was a candidate for a less invasive brain surgery at age 16.

During the EEG, Stevie had to be weaned off her medication so doctors could record her brain activity. Around 3:00 a.m. on the fourth night, she had a full-blown Tonic-Clonic seizure. It was one of the most terrifying moments of my life. I pressed the emergency button, and within seconds, nurses rushed in. She ended up having four seizures when they only needed one. It was so hard to watch.

I remember during one of her seizures in the hospital, she bit her tongue so hard that the side of it turned dark purple. In that moment, I felt completely helpless—watching my baby in pain and unable to do anything to stop it. It broke something in me as a mother, seeing her suffer like that right in front of my eyes.

The machines kept beeping, doctors and nurses moved quickly around her, but everything felt like it was happening in slow motion. All I could focus on was her—my baby—fighting something I couldn't take from her. I wanted to trade places with her. I would have taken every second of that pain if it meant she didn't have to feel it.

After seven days in the hospital, we finally got the results: she was not a candidate for surgery. The spot causing the seizures was too close to areas controlling memory, language comprehension, and auditory processing. The surgery carried the risk of significant memory loss and could have taken away parts of what makes her who she is—possibly leaving her unable to recognize herself or even her own family.

Once again, we were left waiting—and praying. Then everything changed.

My husband, Bobby, took Stevie home early from dinner with my parents so she could get the sleep she needed before school the next day, as sleep deprivation is a known trigger for seizures.

It was August 13, 2019—my cousin Leigh's birthday. Leigh was the labor and delivery doctor when Stevie was born, and Stevie's middle name, "Leigh," was named after her. To be exact, both Stevie and Leigh were named after my maternal grandfather, Lee Brandon—also known as Big Lee, or "Biggie."

That night marked something we had prayed for and longed for all at once.

Her last seizure.

She has never had another seizure since.

Isaiah 40:31 says, "But they who wait upon the Lord shall renew their strength; they shall mount up with wings like eagles, they shall run, and not be weary, they shall walk, and not faint" (KJV). I prayed every single day for God to take those seizures away. And in His perfect timing—not mine—He did. It says several times in the Bible that if you ask, you will receive. Here are a few verses:

Matthew 21:22 "And all things, whatsoever ye shall ask in prayer, believing, ye shall receive" (KJV).

John 14:13-14 " And whatsoever ye shall ask in my name, that I will do, that the Father may be glorified in the Son. If you ask anything in My name, I will do it" (KJV).

John 15:7 "If ye abide in me and my words abide in you, ye shall ask what ye will, and it shall be done unto you" (KJV).

John 16:24 "You haven't done this before. Ask, using my name, and you will receive, and you will have abundant joy" (NLT).

Six months later, Stevie got her driver's license. A dream come true. Today, she is full of life and confidence. She is known in college as "the girl who asks all the questions." She is determined, strong, and thriving.

Looking back, there were so many nights she cried herself to sleep, praying for healing—something I didn't even know at the time, as her mom, that breaks my heart. I wanted to fix it, to take it away, but I couldn't. All I could do was love her and be there.

Now, she lives freely. She can do everyday things without fear. My heart, once broken for 16 years, has finally been made whole.

God healed my daughter!

And I will never stop saying: "Thank you, Jesus. To God be all the glory!"

Epilogue

Now, as a senior in college preparing to graduate in the spring of 2026, I can look back and clearly see how each step of my journey has led me to this moment. In December, I was humbled and overjoyed to receive acceptance into my dream program—the Doctor of Occupational Therapy program at the University of St. Augustine for Health Sciences. I will begin the program in the Fall 2026 term, starting in September, marking the realization of a goal I have worked toward with dedication, faith, and perseverance. This acceptance not only affirms my commitment to occupational therapy but also reinforces my belief that every challenge and redirection along the way has played a meaningful role in shaping the path I am meant to follow.

Stepping into this next is both humbling and emotional, as it represents not only an academic achievement but a personal victory. I am no longer defined by the limitations I once feared; instead, I am empowered by them. I look forward to becoming a clinician who leads with understanding, patience, and heart—someone who sees each individual beyond their diagnosis and helps them rediscover their independence and confidence. This journey has affirmed that I am exactly where I am meant to be, and I am ready to carry everything I have learned into the future with purpose and passion.

Isaiah 40:31 says, "But they that wait upon the Lord shall renew their strength; they shall amount up with wings as eagles; they shall run, and not be weary; and they shall walk, and not faint" (KJV). This verse serves as a reminder that perseverance rooted in faith leads to renewal and purpose. It reassures me that even when the journey feels exhausting, I am being carried forward with strength beyond my own.

"We also rejoice in our sufferings, because we know that suffering produces perserverance; perserverance, character; and character, hope."

Romans 5:3-4

Dedication

This Book is dedicated to Dr. Edwin E. Flournoy & Mrs. Mary E. Flournoy.

They both made a huge impact on my life. They were filled with overflowing kindness and I was blessed to be able to call them my grandparents. They were true followers of Christ and brought everyone closer to God. They constantly reminded me that God is always with us no matter where we go. The people around me shaped me into who I am today. Throughout my life, my grandparents were two constants who were there for me no matter what challenges I faced. I want to share with others that God is real and miracles do happen. Believe in what you pray and your prayers will be answered. Be the light!